ANALYZE THE ANCIENTS

THE Aztecs

Louise Spilsbury

Gareth Stevens
PUBLISHING

Please visit our website, www.garethstevens.com.

For a free color catalog of all our high-quality books,
call toll free 1-800-542-2595 or fax 1-877-542-2596.

Cataloging-in-Publication Data

Names: Spilsbury, Louise.
Title: The Aztecs / Louise Spilsbury.
Description: New York : Gareth Stevens Publishing, 2019. | Series: Analyze the
ancients | Includes glossary and index.
Identifiers: LCCN ISBN 9781538225653 (pbk.) | ISBN 9781538225646 (library bound)
Subjects: LCSH: Aztecs--Juvenile literature. | Mexico--Civilization--Juvenile literature.
Classification: LCC F1219.73 S646 2019 | DDC 972'.01--dc23

First Edition

Published in 2019 by
Gareth Stevens Publishing
111 East 14th Street, Suite 349
New York, NY 10003

© 2019 Gareth Stevens Publishing

Produced for Gareth Stevens by Calcium Creative Ltd
Editors: Sarah Eason and Jennifer Sanderson
Designers: Paul Myerscough and Jessica Moon
Picture researcher: Rachel Blount

Picture credits: Cover: Shutterstock: Yagujinskaja; Inside: Berkeley, University of
California, 1903: p. 41; Flickr: Dennis Jarvis: p. 29; PX Here: p. 37; Shutterstock:
BorisVetshev: pp. 1, 20; Ecco3d: p. 32; Gordon Galbraith: p. 11; Diego Grandi:
p. 5; Dina Julayeva: p. 18; Schlyx: p. 19; Fedor Selivanov: p. 6; Studio Araminta:
p. 15; Maria Uspenskaya: p. 38; Walters Art Museum: p. 39; Wikimedia Commons:
pp. 4, 9, 14, 21, 27, 36; AndonicO: p. 7; Simon Burchell: p. 12; Daderot: p. 24; William
de Leftwich Dodge: p. 43; Bernardino de Sahagún: p. 31; Emmanuel Eslava: p. 22;
The Field Museum Library: p. 28; Geni: pp. 8, 45; Thomas Ledl: p. 42; Madman2001:
p. 40; Joe Ravi: p. 23; Diego Rivera: p. 16; Diego Rivera/ Wolfgang Sauber: p. 35;
Sailko: p. 25; Wolfgang Sauber: p. 17; Einsamer Schütze: p. 26; Jesuit Juan de Tovar:
p. 33; Juan de Tovar: p. 10; Vassil: p. 34; Z-m-k: p. 13; Zuchinni one: p. 30.

Printed in the United States of America

CPSIA compliance information: Batch #CS18GS: For further information, contact Gareth Stevens, New York, New York at 1-800-542-2595.

CONTENTS

CHAPTER 1

The Awesome Aztecs

The Aztecs ruled a vast **empire** in the area that is now central and southern Mexico during the 1400s and early 1500s. At its peak, the Aztec Empire spread over 80,000 square miles (207,199 sq km) between the Pacific and Atlantic coasts of **Mesoamerica**.

Early Aztecs

The word Aztec comes from the name *Aztlán* meaning "White Land." Aztlán was the land in northern Mexico from which experts believe the Aztecs first came. The Aztecs believed that Huitzilopochtli, their god of the sun and war, told their people they should go in search of a new place to settle. They were told that they should build their new city where they saw a sign: an eagle devouring a snake while perched on a flowering cactus. The Aztecs roamed Mexico for about 200 years before they saw that sign on Lake Texcoco in the Valley of Mexico. To avoid conflict with the other peoples who were already there, the Aztecs settled in the swampy land by the lake in a city they called Tenochtitlan.

THE FIRST AZTEC RULER
Acamapichtli was the first ruler of the Aztecs of Tenochtitlan.

Expanding the Empire

Tenochtitlan became a great **city-state** with a rich **society**. The Aztecs were a warrior people and Aztec men were expected to train to fight. The Aztecs expanded the area they ruled outward from Tenochtitlan using their armies to take over new land. They formed an alliance with two other city-states: Texcoco and Tlacopan, fighting together against common enemies. Gradually, Tenochtitlan became the most powerful of the three and the Aztecs became leaders of a wide and great empire. By the reign of the last great Aztec **emperor**, Montezuma II, the Aztecs ruled over almost 6 million people.

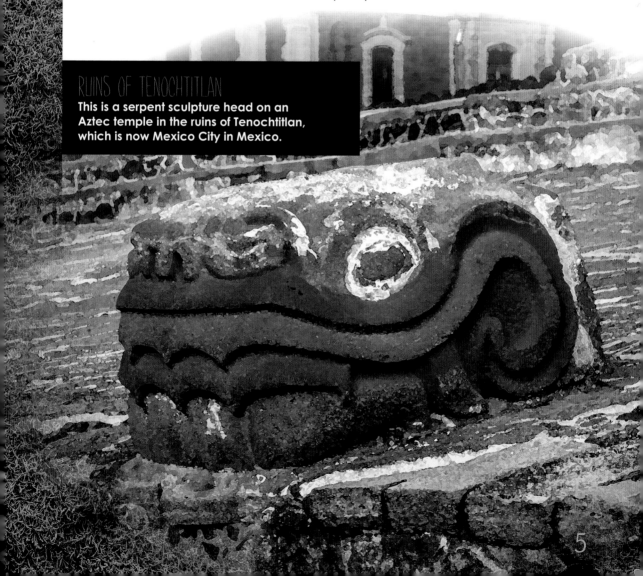

RUINS OF TENOCHTITLAN

This is a serpent sculpture head on an Aztec temple in the ruins of Tenochtitlan, which is now Mexico City in Mexico.

Aztec Society

The rulers or emperors of the Aztecs were the kings of Tenochtitlan, called Huey Tlatoani in the Aztec language. Aztec society was divided into different classes. The king was at the top of the social ladder and everyone else came below him in importance and status.

The Nobles

Directly below the king were the nobles. The noble class consisted of government leaders, commanders, judges, high-level priests, landowners, and lords. When an emperor died, a council of nobles chose the new emperor. The nobles had many privileges. For example, while ordinary people had to pay taxes to the emperor in the form of goods or labor, the nobles did not have to pay taxes. Nobles were also entitled to receive payments from ordinary people. Nobles got their status from their parents, and only nobles were permitted to display their wealth by wearing decorated capes and jewelry.

PROUD NOBLES

This sculpture was made by an Aztec craftsman and depicts a proud noble with an ornate headdress to show his status.

6

The Commoners

Commoners were the ordinary, working people. They lived together in neighborhoods owned by groups of families known as calpulli. Often, a nobleman and some older commoners led the calpulli. The commoner class consisted of farmers, artists, sculptors, doctors, **architects**, **merchants**, and low-level priests. Artists and merchants enjoyed the greatest amount of wealth and respect within this class, and had their own **trade guilds**. The poorer people attended schools to learn their trades and to learn about religion, music, and their language: Nahuatl.

Serfs and Slaves

At the bottom of Aztec society were the serfs and slaves. Serfs did not own or share in owning any land, and did not live in the calpulli. They worked land that the nobles owned. Slaves were criminals and prisoners, or people who were in debt and could not pay their taxes. Most slaves were prisoners taken in war. Slave owners were responsible for housing and feeding their slaves, and slaves generally could not be resold. Slaves were usually granted their freedom when their owner died.

Examining Evidence

We can learn about how ancient people lived and who they were by examining pieces of evidence that they have left behind. We know a lot about the Aztecs by uncovering the remains of the many buildings they built.

Archaeologists at Work

Archaeologists are people who find and dig up these remains. They can study the buildings to learn what tools and building materials the Aztecs used, what their cities were like, and how different people lived. Temples tell them that the Aztecs were religious, and palaces tell them that the Aztec kings were rich and powerful. By digging under temples or following hidden passageways, archaeologists also uncovered **tombs** where rulers were buried with important **artifacts**, such as pots, weapons, and other items that can tell us about past lives. We can also learn about the Aztecs from records made by the Spanish who invaded the country and took over Aztec lands in the sixteenth century.

SYMBOLS OF POWER
Archaeologists find pendants, like this one, which would have been worn across the chest by Aztec leaders. The doubled-headed serpents were symbols of power.

8

Picture Records

The Aztecs also made books called codices. These contain pictures that reveal a lot about their lives. A codex shows scenes from everyday life and is an important record of the way the Aztecs lived. The codices show us that the Aztec emperor in Tenochtitlan did not rule other regions directly. The people were allowed to govern themselves as long as they regularly paid the emperors food and other goods, known as tributes. We know the extent of the empire because some of the tribute items, such as jaguar skins and exotic feathers, came from different regions. Tribute collectors lived in the conquered regions and made sure the payments were made and were on time.

CHAPTER 2

Aztec Beliefs

The Aztecs believed in and worshiped hundreds of gods and goddesses. One reason there were so many gods was that Aztec leaders were happy for the tribes they conquered to continue worshiping their own local gods, as long as they also worshiped Huitzilopochtli, the god of the sun and war and special guardian of Tenochtitlan.

The Power of the Gods

Each Aztec god ruled an aspect of nature or human characteristics. The Aztecs believed that the gods controlled everything in life. Each god had a good side and a bad side, and could make good or bad things happen to people. They believed that to keep the gods happy, they should give thanks to them. That is why the Aztecs built **monuments**, temples, and statues for the gods and performed **sacrifices** as gifts to the gods. Priests made sure that the proper **offerings** and sacrifices were made. They also performed ceremonies in the temples to make sure the gods did not become angry and cause droughts, floods, and other disasters.

THE MAIN GOD

This is an image of Huitzilopochtli, the Aztec god of sun and war. He was one of the most important Aztec gods.

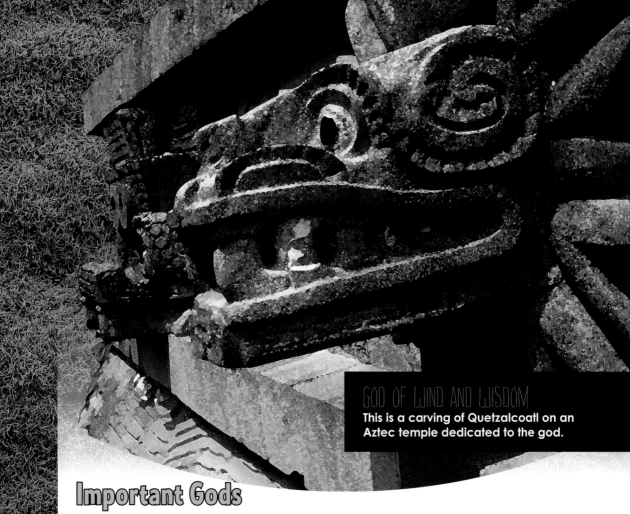

Important Gods

Tlaloc was the god of rain. If happy, he brought the rain that helped crops grow. If angered, he caused storms, thunder, and lightning. He is often shown with fangs and large round eyes. To worship him, priests held ceremonies in which they bathed in the lake, mimicked the calls of water birds, and shook fog rattles to call for rain.

Quetzalcoatl, whose name means "feathered serpent," was the god of wind and wisdom. Aztecs believed he invented calendars and books. As the god of learning, Quetzalcoatl was often worshiped in priest schools linked to temples.

Huitzilopochtli was the Aztec sun and war god, often represented as a hummingbird or an eagle. Aztecs believed he guided them to their home where they built Tenochtitlan. The Aztecs worshiped him by giving offerings of human sacrifices.

Human Sacrifices

As part of their religious ceremonies, the Aztecs sacrificed thousands of people every year. The sacrifices took place in ceremonies on the flat tops of pyramid temples. Afterward, the victims' heads were often displayed like trophies on a large rack.

Why Human Sacrifices?

The Aztecs believed that their gods sacrificed themselves to help the god who sacrificed himself to create the sun. They believed that to repay the gods for their sacrifices, and to keep the sun burning, they had to feed the sun god human blood and hearts. Without human sacrifices, they feared that the sun would stop glowing, and without its warmth and light, everything would die. So to keep life going, the Aztecs regularly killed human victims in ceremonies led by priests. Those who were sacrificed were often slaves or prisoners of war.

SACRIFICIAL KNIFE

Ornate knives made from stone were used to kill victims of sacrifice. This knife is made from a stone called flint. The handle is in the shape of a crouching man covered with small pieces of mosaic stone.

Sacrifice Ceremonies

Masks were an important part of all Aztec ceremonies, including sacrifices. Masks were offered to the gods in a temple or worn by priests and rulers for temple **rituals**. The most powerful masks were made of rare, costly materials, such as the precious blue stone turquoise. Turquoise was sacred, or holy, and represented life. In a sacrifice ceremony to the god Tezcatlipoca, a young man was chosen to live in luxury for a year, and spend his last week singing, feasting, and dancing. Then he climbed to the top of the temple where the priests, wearing fearsome masks to represent the all-powerful god Tezcatlipoca, stretched him over a sacrificial stone and removed his heart.

ANALYZE THE ANCIENTS

This is a mask representing the god Tezcatlipoca. Using your knowledge of the Aztecs, can you answer these questions about the mask?

1. The mask is made from a mosaic of turquoise. Why was turquoise used to make the mask?

2: The mask looks especially frightening. Why do you think it was designed to look scary?

Life After Death

The Aztecs who were sacrificed by priests felt honored to be chosen. It was a great privilege to be sacrificed to the gods because the Aztecs believed this would secure them a place in paradise in the **afterlife**.

The Aztec Afterlife

The Aztecs believed that people went to different places in the afterlife, depending not on how well they lived their life, but on how they died. People killed in sacrifice and warriors who died in battle went to a paradise that was the home of the sun. They helped the sun god rise each morning or fought beside Huitzilopochtli in battle. Women who died giving birth went to paradise and helped the sun god bring in the sun at the end of the day. People who died accidental or violent deaths, such as from lightning or drowning, went to Tlalocan, a paradise ruled by the god Tlaloc. Those who lived a long, healthy life and died of old age or illness, went to Mictlan, the Aztec **underworld**.

THE AZTEC UNDERWORLD
This image from the Aztec codices shows part of Mictlan.

The Aztec Underworld

In the underworld, a person had to travel on a dangerous journey, first by boat, then sinking down under Earth to finally reach the land of the Lord of the Dead. Once they arrived there, these people lived their afterlife serving the Lord of the Dead and living in darkness. Working for the gods in their afterlife was another way the ancient Aztecs tried to keep their gods happy.

Death Masks

After an important or royal Aztec died, death masks made of precious materials were often placed over their faces. The Aztecs believed the death mask would bring them back to life in the afterlife. The masks were symbols that death was a continuation of life. Death masks were often made in the likeness of a god's face. Some were buried with a body or its ashes. Other death masks were offered to the gods or displayed in memory of the dead.

CHAPTER 3

Secrets in Stone

The Aztecs were talented builders and craftsmen who made tools with chisels, hard stones, and blades made from black volcanic glass called obsidian. They made a variety of great buildings and pyramids.

Tenochtitlan

The city of Tenochtitlan was built on an island in Lake Texcoco, which was enlarged by filling in surrounding marshy areas. The city was divided into four sections, called campans, and linked to the mainland by raised roads called causeways. The Aztecs also built a network of canals through the large city so people could travel around it by boat. The Aztecs built a double aqueduct (an artificial channel) that brought freshwater to the city, because the lake water was salty. As the city expanded, the Aztecs had to deal with the sinking soil. To prevent the city from sinking, they used use platforms as **foundations** or drove groups of tightly packed wooden piles into the soil. The Aztecs also built walls to protect the city from flooding, and freshwater **reservoirs** for people to use and to water farm crops.

THE CAPITAL CITY

Tenochtitlan was built around the public plaza, or square, at the center, with temples and pyramids around it. Beyond the center, there were homes, gardens, and farming land. The city expanded until, at its peak, it had more than 200,000 residents.

Palaces

There were many palaces throughout the Aztec empire. Some palaces were for the emperor to live in. Others were in the countryside for him and his family to visit. Some had rooms where the emperor met with his officials to make laws and to plan for governing the empire. There were also halls where courts were held. The palaces usually had many rooms on two stories surrounding a large courtyard. As well as living areas, there would have been libraries, storehouses, a reception area for entertaining guests, and workshops for royal craftsmen.

Montezuma II's palace in Tenochtitlan had hanging gardens, a 10-room aviary filled with different birds, and its own zoo with jaguars, eagles, pumas, foxes, snakes, and hundreds of other animals.

THE KING'S THRONE

This is Montezuma II's throne from his palace in Tenochtitlan. It is carved in the shape of a stepped pyramid and covered in carvings of Aztec symbols, gods, and a picture Montezuma II himself.

Sites of Sacrifice

At the top of the unique Aztec pyramids, there were flat platforms for human sacrifices or temples used for prayers and other rituals. There was often a room that contained a sculpture or an image of the god to whom the temple was dedicated.

Types of Pyramid

There were three main types of Aztec pyramids. The twin stair pyramid had a square-shaped base, two staircases, and two temples at the top, each of which was dedicated to its own particular god. The second type of pyramid was less common: a round pyramid dedicated to the god of wind, Quetzalcoatl. The third type of pyramid had a square-shaped base like the twin stair pyramid, but it was smaller and had just one temple and one set of stairs. These pyramids were mainly found in smaller cities.

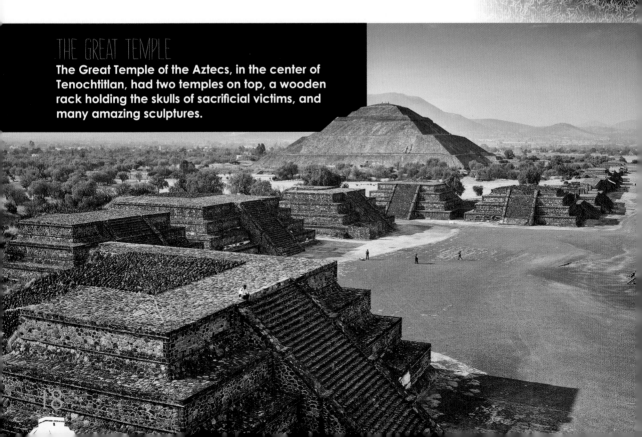

THE GREAT TEMPLE

The Great Temple of the Aztecs, in the center of Tenochtitlan, had two temples on top, a wooden rack holding the skulls of sacrificial victims, and many amazing sculptures.

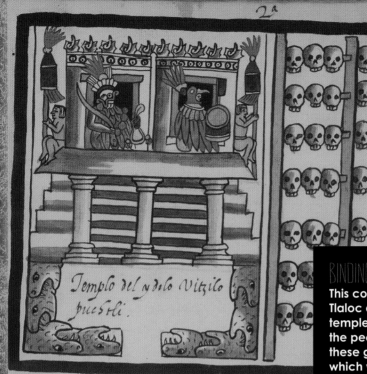

Templo del ydolo Vitzilo pucstli.

BINDING OF THE YEARS

This codex image shows the gods Tlaloc and Huizilopochtli in their temple. It also shows the skulls of the people the Aztecs sacrificed to these gods in religious ceremonies, which were scheduled according to the sun calendar.

How Does It Work?

The Sun Stone is sometimes called the calendar stone because it shows two calendar systems, which are different but linked:

• The 365-day xiuhpohualli calendar describes the days and rituals related to the seasons. It contains 18 months of 20 days each, plus five unlucky days when the Aztecs believed disasters might happen. Around the central image of the sun god, there is a band of 20 different day symbols.
• The 260-day tonalpohualli calendar divides the days and rituals between the gods. Every 24-hour cycle has 1 of 20 day names (such as jaguar or wind) and a number from 1 to 13, because Aztec weeks lasted 13 days.

The Sun Stone calendar worked a little like two linked wheels. By linking the date on one wheel to the other, no date could be repeated for 52 years. The Aztecs believed that when that day came, the universe was in great danger. So every 52 years, they performed a ceremony called the Binding of the Years to prevent disaster.

CHAPTER 4

Work and Trade

The Aztecs had a wide range of jobs and made goods that they were able to trade with peoples far away. Farming was a very important part of Aztec life and a reason for its early success. Using smart farming techniques, the Aztecs were able to build up islands on the swampy land of the lake where they could grow crops. This allowed them to grow more plants than any other farmers in the world at that time, and this success allowed them to feed a growing population.

Floating Farms

The Aztecs grew their main crops on several little islands that they constructed on swampy shallow lake beds. These were called chinampas. They were made by building up thick layers of plants taken from the lake surface, mixed with mud from the bottom of the lake. The Aztecs planted trees and placed stones around the edges of the chinampas to make them stable. They left strips of water, like canals, between them so they could reach their plots by canoe. Aztec farmers had no plows and they did not use animals to help them farm. They relied on hard work and simple tools, such as stone hoes on a wooden stick used to turn the dirt, and a type of shovel with a long handle and a flat stone head.

TRAJINERAS
The Aztecs used flat boats called trajineras to travel among the chinampas, where they grew food crops.

Markets

There were markets all over the Aztec lands, where farmers and other producers could bring their food and other goods to sell. In Tenochtitlan, there were markets throughout the city and a main marketplace where up to 40,000 people could gather to buy and sell goods and food. Officials carefully controlled the prices at the markets, and there were always officials on hand to stop arguments or arrest anyone who tried to steal goods. Some people **bartered** for goods, and some goods functioned as money, including cacao beans, small squares of cotton cloth, small gold nuggets, pieces of tin, and rare feathers.

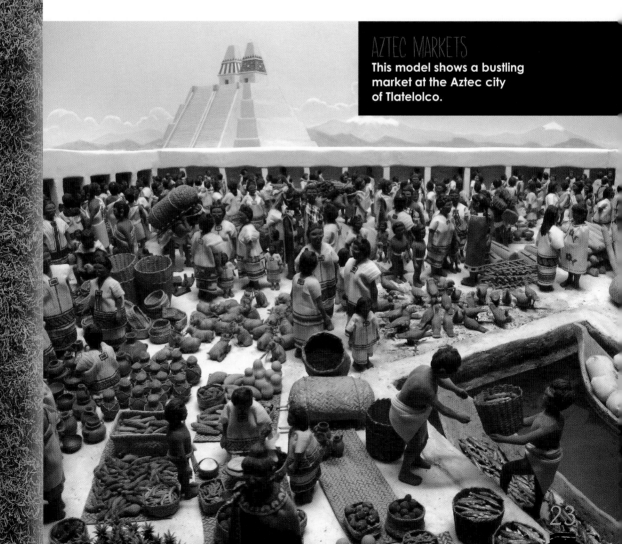

AZTEC MARKETS

This model shows a bustling market at the Aztec city of Tlatelolco.

Merchants and Makers

The Aztecs made a variety of useful and decorative objects for themselves or the temples. They were sold at city markets or traded with other cities.

Merchants on the Move

The Aztec merchants, known as pochteca, traveled vast distances on foot to buy and sell objects. They **exported** luxury items such as jewelry, as well as lake salt and pottery. They **imported** items such as jewelry, textiles, animal skins, rare birds and their feathers, rubber, and a precious stone called jade. They traded goods from as far away as southern New Mexico. Raw materials from Central America arrived in the markets of Tenochtitlan. Merchants were extremely important and could pass their job and land down to their children.

Craftspeople at Work

Aztec potters made simple pots for use in the home and more ornate pottery for rituals. Some craftspeople were skilled at using colorful feathers to make fabulous garments and headdresses for the nobles and royals.

SKILLED POTTERS

The Aztecs usually painted decorations on their pottery in two colors. Here, black and red are used on an orange ceramic plate.

Golden Objects

The Aztecs believed that gold was the sun's **feces** and was therefore sacred, so goldsmiths had a high status among craftspeople. Gold objects, such as labrets, were worn only by high chiefs and royalty. Labrets were a type of plug worn below the lower lip to symbolize the fact that the ruler spoke for the gods. Some labrets were shaped like serpents, creatures that slither on the ground, in water, and among forest trees, just as a god might move on land, in water, and through the sky. These serpent-shaped labrets had a tongue that could move. Labrets would have been worn on ritual occasions and on the battlefield, to strike awe and fear into the hearts of those who saw them.

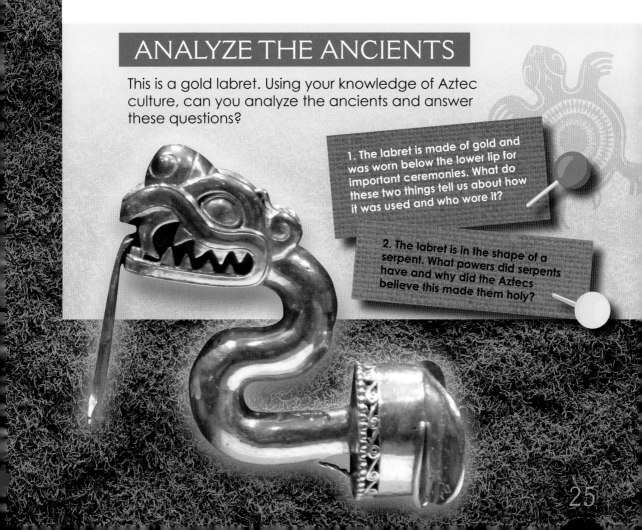

ANALYZE THE ANCIENTS

This is a gold labret. Using your knowledge of Aztec culture, can you analyze the ancients and answer these questions?

1. The labret is made of gold and was worn below the lower lip for important ceremonies. What do these two things tell us about how it was used and who wore it?

2. The labret is in the shape of a serpent. What powers did serpents have and why did the Aztecs believe this made them holy?

The Codex Painters

Merchants needed people to keep records of all their trades and profits. In fact, a lot of paperwork was required to keep the large Aztec Empire running smoothly. Records were kept of many things: the events of the Aztec year, taxes and tributes, temple rituals, lists who belonged to the ruling class, laws and court cases, property, and ownership lists. The codex painters carried out all of this official work.

Codex Pictograms

Being a codex painter was an important job. Most codex painters were nobles who were trained in the calmecacs, which were the advanced schools of the noble class. They had to learn all of the different pictograms the Aztecs used. Pictograms are little pictures that represent different objects. The codex painters had to learn the pictograms and symbols or pictures that represented an idea, too. For example, the idea of death was represented by a picture of a dead body wrapped for burial; night was represented by a black sky and a closed eye; and walking was represented by a trail of footprints.

AZTEC BOOKS

The codices were made of materials such as tree bark, cactus fiber, and animal skins. Strips of these materials up to 39 feet (12 m) long by 7 inches (18 cm) high were cut, and the ends pasted onto thin pieces of wood to form the cover. The strip was folded like an accordion or a map.

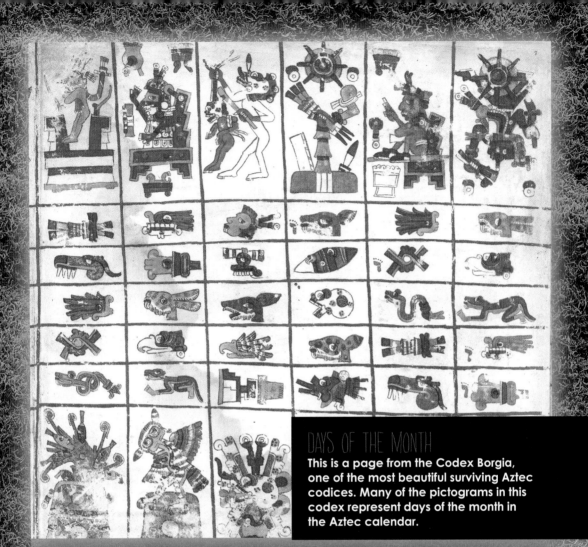

Counting on the Codices

The codex painters also had to learn how to illustrate numbers and how to count. The Aztec number system was based on 20, probably because people have a total of 20 fingers and toes. Numbers 1 to 19 were represented by dots. A little flag or banner represented the number 20, and five bags or banners represented 100. A picture of a feather meant 400, and a bag or pouch of **incense** represented 8,000. The Aztecs used these symbols to count and record all their tributes and trade.

For example, a tribute page showing 18 dots, 5 flags, and 1 pictogram of a shield meant that 118 shields had been sent to the emperor.

CHAPTER 5

War and Warriors

The Aztec Empire was created and controlled by the force and might of its warriors. The Aztec armies conquered new regions and peoples, then helped keep them under control, so the empire could expand and remain powerful.

Aztec Armies

All Aztec men, even the priests, were trained to fight and were expected to take part in battles, at least when they were young. The king was the commander-in-chief of the armed forces. He had a second-in-command and a war council of high-ranking nobles, who planned battles and controlled different units of warriors. The Aztecs did not have a permanent army. Instead, each town was expected to supply up to 400 warriors when needed. Each of these units might be led by one of their own high-ranking warriors or become part of a larger unit of 8,000 men. For major battles, there could be up to 25 units of 8,000 men, totaling 200,000 warriors in all.

AZTEC WARRIORS IN COSTUME

These are Aztec warriors as pictured by a codex painter. The higher the rank, the more elaborate a warrior's costume.

Symbols of Rank

Aztec warriors had different symbols of rank to show how important they were in the army. Some wore ornaments such as lip, nose, and ear plugs. High-ranking Aztec warriors wore feathered capes or suits. If they also wore a feathered headdress that towered above their shoulders, they were high-ranking officers. The best warriors were named jaguar or eagle warriors. Eagle warriors wore helmets with open bird beaks, a costume with eagle wings, and even imitation talons (bird claws) on their legs. The deadliest Aztec warriors were named "the shaved ones." These warriors had one long braid on the left side of their heads and the rest was shaved.

EAGLE WARRIORS

This is a life-size sculpture of an Aztec eagle warrior. It once stood next to the Great Temple of the Aztecs in Tenochtitlan. The eagle was the symbol of the sun god, so the eagle warriors were among the most important of all.

Weapons of War

Older Aztec warriors trained younger warriors in military tactics and how to use weapons and win battles. Later, young men followed armies into battle, carrying bags and supplies, so they could watch and learn from the older warriors. When they finally captured their first prisoner, they were considered warriors. They could then cut off the long braid that had been growing since they were 10 years old.

A Warrior's Weapons

The trainee warriors had to learn to use a variety of weapons. These were made of wood and stone, but never metal. Some were for fighting at close range and others were for longer distance combat. The macuahuitl was a wooden club that had a row of razor-sharp obsidian blades sticking out from the edge. Obsidian could be cut to have dangerously sharp edges, making the macuahuitl a deadly weapon. They also carried spears made from wood that had a blade with an obsidian edge. All Aztec warriors carried a round shield for protection. Some shields were made from jaguar skin and feathers from turkeys, ducks, or colorful tropical birds.

DEADLY MACUAHUITL

This is a modern reconstruction of an Aztec ceremonial macuahuitl.

Long-Range Weapons

Aztec bows and arrows had a sling made from cactus fiber thread, and an arrow made from wood with a sharpened end. An atlatl was a long stick with a grip at one end and a hook to grip the spear at the other. This weapon allowed a warrior to throw a light spear much farther and faster than by hand alone. It had first been used for hunting but could hit an enemy from around 500 feet (152 m) away! Although these weapons were dangerous, the main aim of the Aztec warriors was to capture most of the people they attacked rather than kill them. A warrior who killed instead of captured too many enemies lost respect.

Prisoners and Rewards

Aztec warriors believed that the wars they fought were sacred. They believed that they needed to capture people who could be used as human sacrifices in the temples on top of the pyramids. That would keep the sun moving across the sky and give life to people on Earth.

Rich Rewards

If you were an Aztec commoner, the only way to leave the lower classes and move up in the world was to become a successful warrior. The more prisoners that warriors captured and the braver they fought, the more rewards they would receive. They were rewarded with expensive gifts and honored and praised in public. If they reached the rank of eagle or jaguar warrior, they became nobles. As farmers, they had a share of land they farmed. As successful warriors, they were given shares of other lands that they conquered, which other people worked for them. They could become army leaders and commanders. When not at war, they worked to police the cities and protect merchants on long trips.

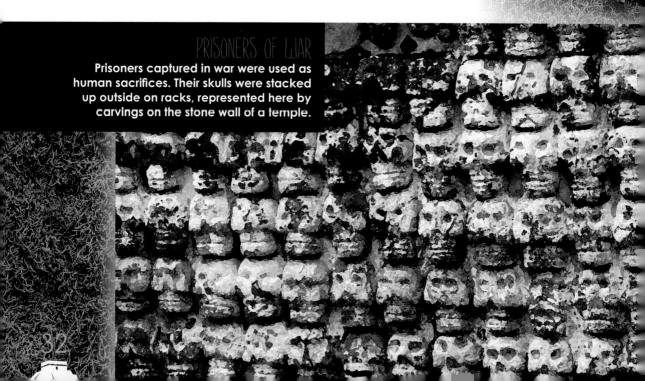

PRISONERS OF WAR

Prisoners captured in war were used as human sacrifices. Their skulls were stacked up outside on racks, represented here by carvings on the stone wall of a temple.

Jaguar Warriors

Aztec warriors who captured a lot of prisoners were rewarded with magnificent eagle or jaguar costumes. The more prisoners they captured, the more elaborate their costumes became to show how successful and brave they were. Jaguar warriors covered their bodies in jaguar skins. The Aztecs regarded the jaguar as the bravest of beasts, and the jaguar represented Tezcatlipoca, god of the night sky. Aztecs also wore jaguar costumes at war because they believed the skins gave them the strength of jaguars during battles. Jaguar warriors often led other warriors into battle so that the enemy, who also thought of jaguars as mighty killers and associated them with magic, would be terrified.

ANALYZE THE ANCIENTS

This codex image shows two warriors in jaguar costumes. Using information you have read about Aztec warriors, can you answer these questions?

1. The jaguar costume was probably the actual skin of a jaguar. What did the jaguar skin mean to the Aztec warrior wearing it and to the enemies he attacked?

2. What is this jaguar warrior holding in his left and right hands? What were they likely to have been made from?

CHAPTER 6

Everyday Life

The houses the Aztecs lived in, the food they ate, and the clothes they wore, all differed depending on the class to which they belonged.

Houses and Homes

Nobles usually lived in large two-story houses made of stone and sundried bricks. The houses had flat roofs, some with a garden on top, and were built around a central courtyard. There were separate living rooms, bedrooms, and kitchens, as well as rooms where servants and slaves lived. Rich people also took a cleansing steam bath every day, in a building where water was poured over hot stones to create steam.

Commoners' houses were much simpler and were often more like huts made of reeds plastered in clay. They often had only one main room and very little furniture. Women and girls wove mats from reeds for the floor. The family slept on thicker versions of these mats. Each home had a garden where the family grew food for itself.

AZTEC MIRRORS

Women began the day by washing and looking into obsidian mirrors, like this one. The women tied up their hair and sometimes wore red paint around their mouths.

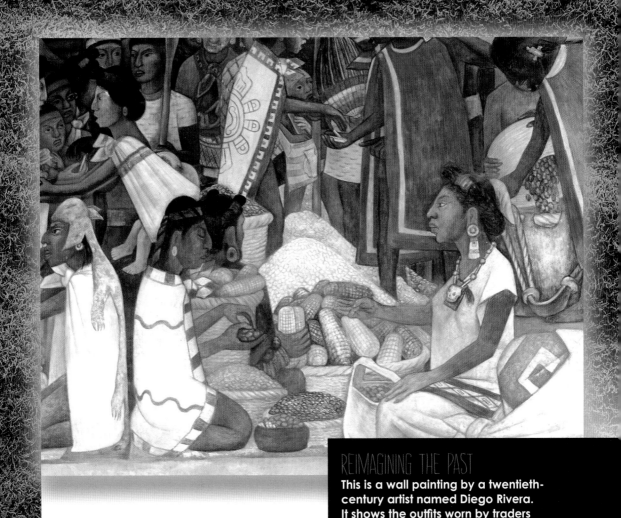

Clothes and Accessories

Slaves would wear only a simple loincloth—a long strip of cloth wrapped to form a short skirt and tied in front. Men also wore triangular cloaks or ponchos over their shoulders. Women wore a shirt, and a skirt wrapped around their hips. These garments were usually made of cotton and undecorated. If people were a little wealthier, they might have **embroidered** or fringed ends. People of high rank wore elaborate costumes, which were colorfully embroidered and often decorated with feathers. Feathers were a clear sign of status. Jewelry such as necklaces, earrings, and bracelets were also worn by the upper classes. Most of the Aztecs walked barefoot everywhere. Only the upper classes and warriors wore sandals.

Family Life

The kind of life you lived in an Aztec family depended on whether you were a girl or a boy. This is because the Aztecs had quite different expectations as to what men and women would do with their lives.

Birth Rituals

When a baby was born, the kind of ritual carried out to mark the occasion was different for boys and girls. For boys, a new shield was placed in his left hand and a newly made arrow was placed in his right hand. Then, a successful warrior buried the baby's **umbilical cord** and the shield and arrow beneath a battlefield. The Aztecs believed these ceremonies would help the boy become a good warrior when he grew up, and show how important warriors were to their survival. If the baby was a girl, the family buried her umbilical cord under the family fireplace. This symbolized that her future was to be a good wife and mother, and take care of her family.

FAMILY TREES

Family was important to the ancient Aztecs. One family had their family tree made from clay.

Growing Up

Most Aztec boys grew up to be farmers and tradesmen, learning the skills of their job from their fathers. Girls learned household skills from their mothers. Education was important to the Aztecs, so children also went to school. The Aztecs were one of the first societies to provide free schooling for all children. However, rich and poor children, boys and girls, as well as slaves, all went to different schools.

Schools were often linked to a temple, so children were taught about their religion and the rules they had to follow. They were also taught the songs and dances that were part of religious ceremonies. Boys also received training to teach them to be good warriors. If a child was particularly good at a subject, such as math, they would be moved into a special class for that subject. The Aztecs knew that it was important to make the most of people's talents.

Food and Drink

The Aztecs ate what they could grow and hunt. This was because they did not raise farm animals. It was easier to grow crops than to catch wild animals, so the Aztecs mainly ate vegetables and grains.

Daily Foods

Rich people ate some meat, such as turkey or wild dog. However, meat was in short supply, so poor people seldom ate it. Poor people did however sometimes eat insects and insect eggs. The Aztecs ground up maize on a grinding stone to make it into flour. They rolled it flat to make tortillas. They also ate corn on the cob and used the corn kernels in soup. They shaped dough into balls, stuffed it with beans and vegetables, and wrapped the balls in maize leaves or husks to make tamales. Beans were soaked in water, cooked until soft, then added to soups and stews. They also ate a wide range of vegetables and fruits, including chili peppers, sweet potatoes, tomatoes, onions, avocadoes, zucchinis, pumpkins, papayas, and pineapples. As well as eating the pineapples, they sometimes hung their spiky tops outside the hut door as a sign that friends were welcome to drop in.

PRICKLY TREATS
The Aztecs also ate the fruit of the prickly pear cactus, which they called nopal.

TRIPOD POTS

Aztec nobles liked their food to be served in this style of shiny, painted pots. This is a tripod pot, with three legs.

Feasts and Treats

The Aztecs ate some foods that are similar to treats people eat today. They used cacao beans to make a kind of hot chocolate, flavored with vanilla. This was the nobles' favorite drink. They crushed peanuts into a thick brown paste, much like the peanut butter people eat today. They also combined cracked nuts with boiled honey to make a kind of peanut brittle candy. They even had chewing gum in the form of chicle, a **resin** extracted from the sapodilla tree. The Aztecs realized that it was also useful as a breath freshener.

Entertainment

The Aztecs worked hard, and warriors were often in danger, but they also knew how to enjoy themselves. They entertained themselves with music, song, dance, and games. Sports were so popular that the best athletes became celebrities.

Music, Song, and Dance

Like so much of Aztec culture, music, song, and dance were closely linked with religion. They were an important part of feasts and ritual ceremonies and celebrations. There were no string instruments, but there were whistles, rattles, trumpets, flutes, and drums. Drums were often made from hollow logs and some were made from turtle shells. Rattles were made from dried gourds, which are large, hard-skinned fruits.

AZTEC DRUMS
Aztec drums were designed to be played horizontally, like this one, or vertically.

Board Games and Sports

Patolli was a board game in which players had to move a set of pebbles from one end of a mat or board to the other end. The mat was divided into four parts with safe and penalty squares. Moves depended on the throws of five beans, which were marked on one side and plain on the other, similar to today's dice. It was a gambling game, and people bet whatever they could afford: blankets, plants, precious stones, gold, food, and in extreme cases, their homes or freedom. Even games had a religious side to them, with players offering prayers to Xochipilli, the god of games, to help them win.

Nobles, high-ranked warriors, and some professional players played ball games on large stone courts. In one game, teams battled to be first to move a heavy, solid-rubber ball through a stone hoop high up on a wall. Ball games were linked to the religious idea of a daily fight between the sun and the darkness, or life and death, and people often gambled on the results.

ANALYZE THE ANCIENTS

This codex image depicts Aztecs playing patolli being watched by Xochipilli, the god of games. Can you answer these questions using your knowledge of the Aztecs?

1. The god of games, Xochipilli, is watching the players. What does this tell us?

2. What do you think the five symbols at the top of the picture are?

Fig. 18. *Juego de patolli (Códice Magliabecchi)*

41

The End of the Aztec Empire

The Aztecs were one of the world's greatest **civilizations**. Their empire came to an end after the Spanish invader Hernán Cortés sailed from Europe to what is now Mexico and conquered the land.

Spanish Invaders

Montezuma II was the Aztec Empire's last ruler, and his reign lasted for 18 years. During that time, Aztec warriors continued to expand the empire, but conquered peoples were becoming increasingly annoyed about paying tributes. When the Spanish arrived in 1519, Montezuma II first welcomed Hernán Cortés and gave him gifts of gold. However, Cortés was not to be trusted. He promised the peoples conquered by the Aztecs that they would be freed from paying tribute if they helped him overthrow Montezuma II. With their help, Cortés and his men, who wore steel armor and carried metal weapons, were able to attack and ultimately defeat Montezuma II and take over the city of Tenochtitlan.

FEATHERED HEADDRESS
This is a feather crown that belonged to the Aztec emperor Montezuma II.

LAST DAYS OF TENOCHTITLAN
This is a nineteenth-century painting depicting the final battle during the Spanish invasion of the Aztec Empire in 1521 and the fall of Tenochtitlan.

Lost Treasures

After the Spanish conquered Montezuma and Tenochtitlan, they went in search of more Aztec treasures. If people tried to resist and stop them from taking their gold, food, or other goods, they were killed. The Spanish melted down many of the treasures and artifacts. For example, the invaders seized vast quantities of gold and melted it into bars that were easier to transport back to Europe. The invaders demolished Aztec temples as a way to force the Aztecs to convert to the Spanish Catholic religion. Aztec libraries containing thousands of works on many subjects, which could have told us even more about their amazing civilization than we know today, were burned to the ground by the Spanish. However, although the empire was gone, the Aztecs did not disappear completely. Tenochtitlan became Mexico City, and many people of Mexican descent have ancestors (relatives who have died) who were Aztecs.

Answers

Did you manage to analyze the ancients? Check your answers against the correct answers on these pages.

PAGE 9

1. By paying tributes to the Aztec emperor, people were allowed to rule themselves.
2. The fact that these tributes include items from far away from Tenochtitlan helps us understand how far the Aztec Empire spread and how far the Aztecs ruled.

PAGE 13

1. Masks were believed to be very powerful and important so this mask is made of turquoise because this stone was very valuable, sacred, and represented life itself.
2. The mask was designed to look scary so that people were in awe of and had respect for the powerful god Tezcatlipoca.

PAGE 19

1. The steps have stone serpent heads to ward off evil spirits.
2. The pyramid was designed to be tall so that commoners could not see the temple from the bottom. Only priests and leaders were allowed to climb the steps to the temple at the top, to be near the gods.

PAGE 25

1. Gold objects, such as labrets, were worn only by high chiefs and royalty. Labrets were worn below the lower lip to symbolize the fact that the ruler spoke for the gods.
2. The Aztecs believed that serpents could move on land, in water, and among trees, just as the gods could travel across land, water, and through the skies. This made serpents sacred, or holy, to the Aztecs.

Answers

PAGE 33

1. The warriors wore jaguar costumes to show they were brave and successful, because the jaguar was a symbol of the power of Tezcatlipoca, the god of the night sky. They also believed the skins gave them the strength of jaguars during battles. When they led warriors into battle, the costumes also scared the enemy.

2. The jaguar warrior is holding a round shield (probably covered in feathers) and a macuahuitl, which was likely made of wood with jagged pieces of sharp obsidian along its edges.

PAGE 41

1. The fact that the god of games, Xochipilli, is shown watching the patolli players reminds us that religion was a part of every aspect of the Aztecs' daily lives, even when they were playing games. It shows they believed that praying and giving offerings to a god could bring them luck and impact everything that happened, even the throw of dice (or beans)!

2. The five symbols at the top of the picture are probably the five beans or patolli that are used as dice and from which the game of patolli gets its name.

Glossary

afterlife life after death

architects people who design and plan buildings

artifacts objects from the past that tell us about people's lives in history

bartered exchanged goods or services for other goods or services

city-state city that with its surrounding area forms an independent state

civilizations settled and stable communities in which people live together peacefully and use systems such as writing to communicate

embroidered decorated with stitches made by sewing

emperor a male ruler or king; an empress is a female ruler or queen

empire a large area of land or a group of countries ruled over by one leader

exported took or sold goods to another country

feces waste matter or droppings

foundations solid structures that support a building from underneath

imported bought and brought goods from another country

incense a substance burned to give off a pleasant smell, often used in religious rituals

merchants people who buy and sell goods

Mesoamerica the name for the region of Mexico and Central America where the Maya lived

monuments statues, buildings, or other structures made to remember an event, time, or person

offerings things that people give as part of a religious ceremony or ritual

reservoirs artificial lakes for collecting and storing water

resin a sticky substance produced by trees

rituals ceremonies performed for religious reasons

sacrifices animals or people killed to honor a god or gods

society a large group of people living together in an organized way, often sharing a religion, making decisions about how to do things, and sharing work that needs to be done

tombs buildings where dead people are put to rest

trade guilds groups of people who work together at the same trade

umbilical cord the tube that connects a baby in the womb to its mother and supplies it with nutrients

underworld the mythical world of the dead

For More Information

Books

Croy, Anita. *What Became of the Aztec Cities?* (Mysteries in History: Solving the Mysteries of the Past). New York, NY: Cavendish Square Publishing, 2017.

Mahoney, Emily. *Ancient Aztec Culture* (Spotlight on the Maya, Aztec, and Inca Civilizations). New York, NY: PowerKids Press, 2016.

Niver, Heather Moore. *Ancient Aztec Daily Life* (Spotlight on the Maya, Aztec, and Inca Civilizations). New York, NY: PowerKids Press, 2016.

Owens, Lisa L. *A Journey With Hernán Cortés* (Primary Source Explorers). Minneapolis, MN: Lerner Publications, 2017.

Websites

There are fun facts about the Aztecs at:
www.dkfindout.com/uk/history/aztecs

Learn more about the amazing Aztecs at:
www.history.com/topics/aztecs

There are lots of Aztec topics to choose from at:
www.historyonthenet.com/tag/aztec

Publisher's note to educators and parents: Our editors have carefully reviewed these websites to ensure that they are suitable for students. Many websites change frequently, however, and we cannot guarantee that a site's future contents will continue to meet our high standards of quality and educational value. Be advised that students should be closely supervised whenever they access the Internet.

Index